The Making of a Prophet

by

Henry F. Butler, Jr.

Copyright © 2010 by Henry F. Butler, Jr.

The Making of A Prophet

All rights reserved solely by the author. The author guarantees all contents are original and do not infringe upon the legal rights of any other person or work. No part of this book may be reproduced in any form without the permission of the author. The views expressed in this book are not necessarily those of the publisher.

Cover design by: Latoya Bady,
                  TBady Graphic Designs
                  Chicago Illinois
                  Tbady@live.com

Cover Art by: Carl E. Lockwood

Life To Legacy, LLC
www.Life2legacy.com
P.O Box 1239
Matteson, IL 60443
(877) 267-7477

ISBN number: 9780983131717

Printed in the United States of America

Literary consultation services provided by: Dennis James Woods

Table of Contents

Preface   i
Acknowledgements   v

Chapter One
A Baby Is Born   1
The Baby Is Named   10
The Church   22

Chapter Two
The Big Day   30
The Beginning of The Mission   36
David Visits the Prison   43

Chapter Three
The Mission   48
Confessions   62

Chapter Four
The Blessings   66
David Comes Home   85
Families Reunited   90

Preface

Not long ago, I was at home immersed in the development of a product for my Christian gifts and cards production company, named Butler's Scrolls of Love. I was adding the finishing touches to a greeting card, when suddenly the Lord began to impart into me a storyline about a woman who was nine months pregnant. At first, I was surprised by this amazing impartation, because I didn't know of any pregnant women. Neither did I understand the reason the Lord would impart such a thing to me. However, this storyline, this dramatic theme that had now completely captured my heart, began to come to life in a wonderful way. It was at this moment that what had started out as just a mere thought, a fleeting daydream, had now become a calling, a divine charge that once I picked it up, I was determined to run with all the way.

On a regular basis, the Lord would begin to impart greater details to me about this story which started developing into a gripping inspirational drama. New aspects of this work began coming to me at different times and places. Sometimes I would be in my bathroom, in my car, or even at the park when I would begin to record on my tape recorder what the Lord was giving me.

Ironically, my initial thought about this drama was not to write a book. I felt as if the Lord was giving me an outline for a powerful Christian film. So day after day, week after week, month after month for an entire year, I received this powerful dramatic work from the Lord.

Soon, I began to share with others what the Lord was giving me. Everyone who I talked to was just as intrigued by this amazing story as I was. One woman even started weeping as she heard aspects of this powerful story. Everyone started encouraging me by saying they couldn't wait to read the story, and that's when the Lord used Pastor Jerome Gilbert to suggest that this dramatization be written not in a book, but in screenplay format. Immediately, that resonated within my spirit and I was in agreement with what the pastor prophetically spoke to me about the style of this project.

"A book in screenplay form," I pondered. I knew nothing about writing a book or a screenplay, nor did I know anyone who did. However, what I did know was that God was going to provide the way. One day after leaving a local hospital where I had been praying for someone, I was going to my car and a woman saw my T-shirt, which had a menorah on the back of it, and she commented that it was of Hebrew origin. She then went on to say that, she was a screenwriter. That's when I told her about this project and how I had everything on tape. She told me that I had a long way to go, and perhaps I should get a book on screenplay development or maybe even visit a local college to gain some knowledge and insight on writing a screenplay.

Though I welcomed her input and saw this as another step in the right direction, I have known the Lord to be my Provider all my life, and I felt that since He was the one who gave me this task of bringing this dramatic work to fruition, then He would be the one who would supply all my needs to complete this task.

One day an acquaintance of mine, a seamstress by the name of Sister Mary Posten, told me that her son, Kevin Posten, writes screenplays. When I heard this, I was elated. Soon after that, Kevin transcribed what I had recorded into a screenplay. And Sister Mary's other son, Carl E. Lockwood, is the gifted artist who did the cover art for this book. Just as I had felt in my spirit, God came through and provided all my needs according to His riches in glory.

It is my deepest desire that all who read this anointed dramatic work would be strengthened, encouraged, delivered and empowered to walk by faith and not by sight, and to be fully lead by the Spirit of God. In the book of Proverbs, the bible says, "In all thy ways acknowledge Him, and He shall direct thy paths."

So please enjoy this book given to me by the Lord entitled: *The Making of a Prophet.* This is a prophetic book done in script form about a baby who was thrown away, saved by God, then protected and raised up to touch the hearts of many for His divine glory.

Acknowledgements

I would like to thank God for all of the individuals that have been a blessing to me in the development of this project and have contributed to my life as a servant of God. Without these caring people, I could not have completed this great work for the Lord. I pray their continued blessing and strength in the Lord.

Sister Gloria Tolliver
Sister Fannie Walker
Mother Georgia Jones, affectionately known as *Momma* Jones
Veronica Tolson

My children: Antwion Butler, Lolita Chandler, Kynora Rogers, DuPree Butler
To my granddaughter Sade Walker, and my sisters Edna Butler and Rachel Gladman who proofread this book. And to all of my wonderful grandchildren, I love you all dearly.

My niece, Bria Butler who transcribed this work from audio

Alice Caldwell
Brother Bob Boyce
Larry Colon
Keith Gregory

Dr. Dennis James Woods, General Editor, Life to Legacy Publishers for all of his contributions and expertise

Chapter One

A Baby is Born

The story begins in an urban neighborhood of a large Midwestern city. It's early Monday morning, about 6:15. The city is just about to come to life as early morning commuters begin to scurry to their places of employment. Traffic is light. Only a few pedestrians are on Grace Street on this seemingly ordinary morning. The rising sun has cleared the treetops, illuminating the golden hazy skies. According to the forecast, it's going to be a nice day, sunny with only partly cloudy skies. In the distance, about halfway down the street is the Grace Community Motel, a nice establishment founded by Deacon Charles Seeman as a place where visiting relatives and friends of church members could stay in a wholesome Christian environment.

However, in this particular incidence, there is a woman who has come to this tranquil motel in distress – she's nine months pregnant and experiencing sharp labor pains. The time has come, she's ready to deliver. It was only a few hours earlier, at 3:15, that she entered this quiet motel room. However, she didn't have to check-in with the attendant because she already had been given the key to the room.

Henry F. Butler, Jr.

When she arrived, she was wearing a long oversized trench coat with a red scarf tied around her head. She carried an ominous black suitcase into her room. She looked around behind her before entering the room, to check to see if someone had followed her. After entering the room, she noticed that the lights were on. "He must have left the lights on," she thought. Quickly, she reached over and turned off the lights and then pulled down the window shade. She laid the black suitcase down on the bed and took out a thick blanket and spread it out on the bed as best she could. She propped up two pillows for support and carefully eased onto the bed and laid back.

Although she did everything she could to be comfortable, it didn't really matter; the labor pains were relentless, coming one after the other. For two agonizing hours she tossed and turned, waiting for her baby to come. Now exhausted, her eyelids have become heavy, but all she can do is nod intermittently. She can't really sleep – the labor pains are too intense. Each passing minute is like an hour. As the clock on the wall keeps ticking, the time draws closer to the hour of delivery.

At the same time, a garbage truck has just passed through the intersection of 34th and Layland, turning west onto Grace Street. The truck stops sporadically, picking up garbage along the way, slowly moving closer to the Grace Community Motel. There's a garbage collector hanging on the back of the truck. His name is Sam. Sam is in a jovial mood and is praising the Lord, singing one of his favorite songs, *"I'm a Soldier in the Army of the Lord."* He wasn't always the jovial type though, because he used to be a tough and callous street fighter. But during an outdoor crusade two years ago, he gave his life to the Lord, and now he's fighting a different fight: the good fight of faith in Christ Jesus. That's why he always sings his favorite song:

> **Sam**
> **(giving God the praise)**
> I'm a soldier in the army of
> the Lord. I'm a sanctified
> soldier in the army...

As he continues to hum the song, Josh, the driver, joins in and begins

The Making of a Prophet

to play his harmonica. Josh also loves the Lord with all his heart, and he likes kidding around. Before Josh gave his life to the Lord, he was a racecar driver and mechanic. But one day while racing his car, he flipped three times and crashed into a fence. Miraculously, he made it out alive. Since he realized that God spared him, he gave his life to the Lord during an outdoor soul-winning crusade that Pastor John was holding. Josh no longer races cars for a living because the Lord blessed him with a job driving trucks for the city.

Meanwhile, back at the Grace Community Motel, the woman delivers her own baby. It's a boy. Quickly, she grabs a pair of scissors that she placed on the nightstand. She cuts the umbilical cord and then ties it off. When she gets up from the bed, she stumbles because she's weak. She goes into the bathroom to clean up, closing the door behind her. When the woman comes out, she goes over to the bed, removes her blanket, folds it back up and places it back into her bag. She takes her newborn and places him into a garbage bag. She attempts to contain her emotions, but a tear slips out and rolls down her face. She opens the door and the sunlight practically blinds her. She's forced to shield her eyes as she hurries to the rear of the Grace Community Motel, where the garbage cans are located. As she approaches the garbage cans, she looks around to see if anyone is looking. She opens the lid, places her nameless newborn baby in the garbage can, and gasps as she closes the lid. A car with a shadowy figure behind the wheel pulls up, and she hurriedly gets into the car. The sound of the slamming car door gives way to the piercing sound of screeching tires as the car speeds away.

By this time, the garbage truck is making its way through the alley to empty the garbage cans behind the motel. Sam takes a garbage can and dumps it into the back of the truck. Then he pulls the lever to engage the compactor. Right as the compactor is coming down, God sends a breeze that opens the bag the woman just placed in the can. At that very instant, Sam sees the helpless infant in his would-be plastic bag tomb. Immediately, he pulls the lever to stop the compactor. Then he yells out:

Sam
Oh my God! There's a baby
in this garbage bag!

This strong muscular man shows unusual gentleness as he gingerly places both of his hands under the garbage bag and carefully removes the bag from amongst the garbage heap. Then he pulls back the bag from around the baby's head. The baby is motionless and its face has an eerie bluish color.

> **Josh**
> Sam, don't joke like that man. I don't play like that!

But Sam doesn't respond to him. Josh then says:

> **Josh**
> You're playing right? SAM!

But Sam still doesn't respond to him. Josh opens the door, hops down from the driver's seat, and hurries toward the back of the truck. He sees Sam holding the baby, still in the garbage bag with its little head protruding. Sam is trying to get the baby to start breathing. Josh cries out:

> **Josh**
> Oh Lord!

> **Sam**
> Let's get inside the truck.

They run around and get into the truck. Sam says to Josh:

> **Sam**
> Drive to the nearest hospital and floor it. Don't stop for nothing!

Sam gently rests his bible on the baby, then closes his eyes and looks to heaven and prays:

The Making of a Prophet

Sam
Lord! Give this baby a miracle. I know you can do it, Lord.

Josh hurriedly backs the truck out of the alley and pulls into traffic. Josh floors the gas pedal and the truck begins speeding down Grace Street. Cars are frantically swerving to avoid colliding with the truck. A police officer sees the garbage truck speeding through traffic. He turns on his lights and siren and immediately begins in hot pursuit. Josh looks through the side view mirror and sees the police car closing fast, with its lights flashing and siren blaring away. But the garbage truck is not stopping for anything. Josh then says:

Josh
(excited and anxious)
Look who's behind us.

Sam then looks through the side view mirror and sees the police car tailing closely behind them. Sam responds:

Sam
Oh, Lord. Turn on the hazard lights and keep going. We're not that far from the hospital.

Josh turns on the hazard lights and continues speeding through the traffic. Soon the garbage truck makes its way to the hospital, screeching to a halt at the emergency room entrance. Sam gets out of the truck and rushes into the emergency room. The baby's body is still covered up. Only its little head protrudes from the ominous plastic bag. The ER doctors and nurses see what is going on, so they run over to Sam. Sam hands the baby over to them and they immediately initiate emergency medical procedures. As they close the curtains surrounding the operating table, the admissions receptionist beckons Sam to come over to her:

>Henry F. Butler, Jr.

> **Receptionist**
> Can we get your name and the information concerning the baby?

Sam obliges and goes over to the receptionist, while the medical team is busy attempting to resuscitate the baby. They try emergency breathing again and again, but the baby is still not responding. After several minutes have elapsed, the doctor shakes his head and says:

> **Dr. Jensen**
> Call it.

The ER nurse looks at her watch and says:

> **ER Nurse**
> Seven thirty-five a.m.

Dr. Jensen turns to walk away as the nurse pulls a sheet over the baby's lifeless body. Now, Dr. Jensen prepares himself to deliver the bad news to Sam. The Doctor walks over to the receptionist to have her page Sam, who has momentarily stepped out of the emergency room:

> **Dr. Jensen**
> Could you page the gentleman who brought this baby in, please?

> **Receptionist**
> Yes, right away, Dr. Jensen. Mr. Sam Brown, could you please return to the emergency room admissions desk?

Sam hears the page and immediately returns:

The Making of a Prophet

Sam
I'm Sam Brown. You paged me?

The receptionist replies:

Receptionist
Yes. Dr. Jensen would like to have a word with you.

Sam goes over to the doctor, who is writing in a chart. Dr. Jensen looks up at him, takes a deep breath and says:

Doctor
Mr. Brown, I'm sorry. We did all that we could do to resuscitate him, but we couldn't bring him back. I'm sorry Mr. Brown, I'm really sorry.

Sam defiantly shakes his head no, and says:

Sam
No…No! I don't receive that! I still believe that God will give this baby a miracle. The Lord didn't have me find and rescue this baby for nothing. I don't care what y'all say. God has the last say so!

He then turns and walks out of the hospital. Meanwhile, the police car has pulled behind the garbage truck. The police officer exits his squad car and walks over to the garbage truck. He steps onto the truck and recognizes the driver:

Officer Tim
I should have known it was you. What happened *this* time?

Josh begins to tell the police officer how Sam had found a baby discarded in a garbage can behind the Grace Community Motel, and how they had rushed to the hospital to save this baby's life. The police officer grabs Josh's hand, his ticket book falling to the ground, and he begins to pray that the Lord would give this baby another chance. Then Officer Tim picks up his ticket book and goes inside the hospital to check on the baby while Sam and Josh get back into the truck and continue their route.

Meanwhile, an elderly woman called Mother Brooks is also at the ER. She had become very ill while at home and needed to see a doctor. While in the ER, she sees what transpires with the baby. Her heart is very heavy over this tragic incident and she begins to feel great compassion for the baby. The more she thinks about it, the more she is disturbed in her spirit. Tears begin to fall from her eyes as she quietly begins to intercede on the baby's behalf. Then suddenly, she gets up and walks over to the admissions desk and asks:

Mother Brooks
Where's the restroom? Can you please direct me to the restroom?

The receptionist points in the direction of the restroom. Mother Brooks goes inside the restroom and closes the door. She falls to her knees, lifts up her hands to heaven and begins praying a fervent prayer on the baby's behalf:

The Making of a Prophet

Mother Brooks
Lord, you specialize in using trash. When things don't seem to be any good, you turn it around and use it for your glory. Lord, I pray that you send life into this baby, in the name of Jesus.

Mother Brooks then stands to her feet and looks into the mirror as she wipes away tears from her face. At the same time, back in the ER the baby suddenly coughs and begins to cry aloud. Everyone hears it. The startled nurses rush over to see the baby who just came back to life. They can't believe their eyes.

Nurse
Oh My God, HE'S ALIVE! HE'S ALIVE!

While this is occurring, Mother Brooks comes out of the restroom and walks over to the admissions desk as the receptionist calls her to see the doctor. Mother Brooks smiles and says:

Mother Brooks
I'm alright now, because the Lord has heard my cry.

Mother Brooks then leaves out and heads home.

Henry F. Butler, Jr.

The Baby is Named

After the initial shock, the excited nurses realize that the baby needs a name. They want an appropriate name. One of the nurses says:

> **Nurse**
> We should name him David, because he overcame some tremendous odds.

So they all agree that David will be his first name. However, baby David still needs a last name. One of the nurses mentions that she attends the Welcome Home Church just down the street, where Pastor Bowen is the pastor. He's a wonderful man of God who flows in a prophetic anointing. Everyone likes the idea of Bowen for a last name, so they name the baby David Bowen. Since no one knows who David's mother or father is, they have to call the Child Welfare Department. David is now placed in foster care.

"Four Years Later"

One day while Mother Brooks is driving to church for noon day prayer, God speaks to her, saying:

> **Voice of God**
> How is the baby that was taken out of the trash?

> **Mother Brooks**
> Lord, is he doing well? I don't even know where they are keeping the child. I don't even know what the child's name is.

Mother Brooks arrives at the church. She goes in, and everyone is gathered for prayer. One of the members says:

Congregate
I'd like to request a special prayer for David Bowen. He's the baby that was taken out of the garbage four years ago. Although he was adopted, the adoption soon failed and they ended up bringing David back. He is now in a place for abandoned children, so I'm requesting special prayer for him.

After church ends, Mother Brooks says to Sister Molly, who is also a nurse who works at the hospital:

Mother Brooks
Where are they keeping David?"

Sis. Molly
114 Holmes Street.

Mother Brooks leaves and drives to the group home where they're keeping David. She goes in and asks to see young David. They look, but they can't find the child. Then suddenly, there is a small hand stretching forth and reaching up, grabbing hold of Mother Brooks' hand. Mother Brooks looks down and sees the child. He is staring up at her and she's staring down at him. Like a magnet, they are drawn together. Mother Brooks says to young David:

Mother Brooks
How are you doing today young David?

Young David responds:

Henry F. Butler, Jr.

> **David**
> (Holding on to her hand)
> Fine. Do you want me to sing my song to you?

Mother Brooks lovingly obliges David:

> **Mother Brooks**
> Yes young David. Sing your song to me.

Young David begins to sing *"Jesus Loves the Little Children of the World."* David's sweet sounding little voice touches Mother Brooks' heart, causing her to weep. When he finishes singing his song, Mother Brooks wipes the tears from her eyes and says to young David:

> **Mother Brooks**
> That was so good, young David. You sing very well. Sit here in this chair for a moment, while I talk to the lady at the desk.

Young David gets up in the chair and sits down. Mother Brooks walks over to the lady at the desk, whose name is Ms. Stills, and says:

> **Mother Brooks**
> Miss, who do I have to see about taking care of David?

She replies:

> **Ms. Stills**
> May I ask who's going to be taking care of David?

Mother Brooks replies:

The Making of a Prophet

> **Mother Brooks**
> Me…I'd like to take care of him.

Ms. Stills frowns slightly and responds, saying:

> **Ms. Stills**
> Oh no. I'm sorry, but that's not possible. He's better off staying here with us until someone that has the resources to provide all the care he needs takes him.

A heartbroken Mother Brooks turns around and walks back over to David and says:

> **Mother Brooks**
> Young David, I have to be going now. But I promise I'll be back to see you.

David hops up out of the chair and embraces her saying:

> **David**
> Don't go! Please don't go!

Mother Brooks, holding back the tears responds:

> **Mother Brooks**
> But I have to be going, young David. I'll be back to see you soon as I can.

David is heartbroken. He doesn't want her to leave. He starts to cry, drops his little head and lets her go. Mother Brooks is choked up, but wants him to remain hopeful:

Henry F. Butler, Jr.

Mother Brooks
David, look up at me.

He lifts his head back up. Mother Brooks says to young David:

Mother Brooks
I'll be back to see you, young David. I'll be back.

As she turns around to leave, the director, Mr. Murray, walks past and sees Mother Brooks. Mr. Murray says to Mother Brooks:

Mr. Murray
It's so good to see you, Mother Brooks. Didn't we have a good service at church Sunday? When Pastor John gave the altar call, there had to be at least fourteen people that came up and gave their lives to the Lord. You know the Lord had to be pleased at that. And I want to thank you again, Mother Brooks, for praying for my wife and children. By the time I made it home from church, the flu that they had was gone. My wife was up cooking and the children were playing. But, anyway, what brings you out here today and why are you crying?

Mother Brooks replies:

> **Mother Brooks**
> I came to see if I could take young David home with me and take care of him. But the lady at the desk told me no. She said he's better off staying here until someone else comes who can afford to take care of him.

Mr. Murray is perturbed by this report and responds angrily:

> **Mr. Murray**
> What! She said that to you?

Mother Brooks emphatically replies:

> **Mother Brooks**
> Yes, she did.

Mr. Murray wants to get to the bottom of this matter right away. He tells Mother Brooks:

> **Mr. Murray**
> Please come with me.

Mr. Murray and Mother Brooks walk over to the desk where Ms. Stills is sitting. Mr. Murray is going to tactfully pull some strings. He disarms Ms. Stills by saying:

> **Mr. Murray**
> Ms. Stills, I'd like you to meet a very good friend of mine, one of the mothers at my church...Mother Brooks.

Ms. Stills is visibly shocked, and awkwardly says:

Henry F. Butler, Jr.

Ms. Stills
Oh...I'm glad to meet you, Mother Brooks.

Mother Brooks is accommodating and replies:

Mother Brooks
Thank you. I'm glad to meet you, too.

Mr. Murray then informs Ms. Stills about his desires concerning David, saying:

Mr. Murray
My prayers have been answered concerning David. Mother Brooks drove all the way over here just to inquire about becoming his caregiver.

Ms. Stills replies:

Ms. Stills
Uhh yeah, but aren't there some state requirements that need to be met first?

Mr. Murray is very aware of all the state regulations for becoming a foster parent. He acknowledges Ms. Stills' concerns by responding:

Mr. Murray
Yes. You're right. We can't overlook those.

Ms. Stills then says to Mr. Murray:

The Making of a Prophet

Ms. Stills
Yeah, cause you know how those state licensing reps are. They want every "I" dotted and every "T" crossed.

Mr. Murray suddenly gets an idea, and asks Mother Brooks:

Mr. Murray
Mother Brooks...Do you still have your certificate for the course that Pastor John's church hosted a couple of months ago for becoming a foster parent?

Mother Brooks
Yes I do. Got it right here in my bible. You told us that we should put it in a safe place cause you never know when we would need it, and it looks like that time is now.

Mr. Murray then turns to Ms. Stills and asks:

Mr. Murray
You know that position that opened up when Ms. Bernice retired?

Ms. Stills
Yeah, but she was a supervisor. Is that the position you're talking about?

Henry F. Butler, Jr.

> **Mr. Murray**
> Yes, that's the one. I think I made my decision on who I want to fill it.

Ms. Stills isn't sure what's really happening. She can't hide her uncertainty. Mr. Murray turns to Mother Brooks, smiles, and announces to Ms. Stills:

> **Mr. Murray**
> Meet your next supervisor...Mother Brooks!

Ms. Stills is flabbergasted. She can't believe her ears and responds sharply:

> **Ms. Stills**
> What!

> **Mr. Murray**
> Oh yes. That's right.

Mr. Murray then informs Mother Brooks:

> **Mr. Murray**
> As supervisor, you have the right to take David home with you today and take care of him until your foster care license clears the state. You can even do most of your work at home and at church. When your license comes back, you can make the choice of who you want to fill your current position. Will you accept the job?"

Mother Brooks joyfully responds:

Mother Brooks
Yes, I'll be glad to.

Mr. Murray
Then it's settled. We'll get David's things together and you can take him home with you today.

Ms. Stills' attitude has suddenly changed. Now she's offering Mother Brooks assistance:

Ms. Stills
I'll be happy to get David's things for you and take them out to your car.

Ms. Stills gets David's things from his room and they all walk out to the car. Mr. Murray opens Mother Brooks' door and Ms. Stills places David's things in the back seat. Ms. Stills asks Mother Brooks:

Ms. Stills
Is there anything else I can do for you?

Mother Brooks answers:

Mother Brooks
No. That will be all, and I thank you for helping us.

Mother Brooks suddenly becoming her supervisor has turned the tables on Ms. Stills in a way that she didn't expect. She is now experiencing deep conviction. So she musters up some humility and says:

Henry F. Butler, Jr.

Ms. Stills
I feel so bad. I'm sorry for what I said to you. Is there any way that you can forgive me?

Mother Brooks is understanding and gently responds:

Mother Brooks
The Lord forgave us of what we've done wrong. The least we can do is forgive one another.

Ms. Stills
Oh, I appreciate that. Thank you so much.

Mr. Murray opens the car door for Mother Brooks and waits for her to get in. He smiles and closes the door. Ms. Stills walks David around to the car and opens the door for David to get in. David kindly says:

David
Thank you.

Mother Brooks rolls down the car window and says to Mr. Murray:

Mother Brooks
Deacon Murray, I thank you for all you have done.

Mr. Murray
I know the Lord could not have chosen a better person than you to take care of David.

The Making of a Prophet

Mother Brooks
Praise the Lord. Yes, God knows what's best.

Mr. Murray then makes a request of Mother Brooks:

Mr. Murray
Could you just keep me and my family in your prayers?

Mother Brooks
You know I will. And Ms. Stills, you have a blessed day.

Deacon Murray returns the blessing:

Mr. Murray
You have a blessed day too.

Mother Brooks and David both give a warm smile and wave goodbye. Mr. Murray and Ms. Stills are very happy for them and with bright smiles they joyfully return their wave as Mother Brooks' car slowly pulls away.

Henry F. Butler, Jr.

The Church

Mother Brooks takes David to church to see the pastor because she wants him to have a male mentor in his life. When they arrive, the pastor is enjoying first lady Elisabeth's rendition of *"Jesus Loves the Little Children,"* as she sings and plays the piano. Some years ago, she lost her sight after her son left home, and she never regained it. As soon as Mother Brooks enters the sanctuary, she greets the pastor and the first lady:

Mother Brooks
God bless you Pastor John and First Lady Elisabeth. How y'all doing today?

First Lady
We are doing just fine. And how about yourself?

Pastor John says to Mother Brooks:

The Pastor
You know God is taking good care of me, cause He gave me Elisabeth. She's such a precious gift. I just love her so, and she hasn't ceased to amaze me yet.

First Lady blushes and chuckles, saying:

First Lady
Oh, John.

Pastor John looks over at Mother Brooks and notices that she has company:

The Making of a Prophet

The Pastor
Mother Brooks, who's that little feller you have with you today?

Mother Brooks
This is David Bowen.

The Pastor
Well we've got the same last name, so he must be a good young feller.

Mother Brooks
Yeah, he's a very special child and that's exactly why I brought him here tonight.

Mother Brooks then tells the pastor what's on her mind:

Mother Brooks
David is going to be staying with me now, but there are things about being a man that I can't teach him. He needs a positive male role model in his life. So I brought David here to meet you and First Lady Elisabeth, to ask you if you could please be his mentor.

The Pastor
I would love to be David's mentor. You know the Bible says that David was a man after God's own heart.

First Lady Elisabeth is delighted and says:

> **First Lady**
> Pastor John's a very good man. He'll make a fine mentor.

Right after the pastor agrees to become David's mentor, the First Lady calls for David:

> **First Lady**
> David, come over here, sweetie.

David comes over to her as she requested, climbs up on the piano stool and says:

> **David**
> I know that song.

They begin to sing a few verses of *"Jesus Loves the Little Children."* After they finish, Mother Brooks calls David and says:

> **Mother Brooks**
> David, we have to be going now.

David gives the first lady a hug and she says:

> **First Lady**
> There's something special about this child.

> **The Pastor**
> David is a prophet in the making.

What the pastor just said strikes a chord with Mother Brooks, who responds by saying:

The Making of a Prophet

Mother Brooks
I knew there was something special about this child.

The Pastor
God's going to use him mightily one day.

Mother Brooks
You hear that, young David? God is going to use you, son.

With a smile on her face and tears of joy beginning to flow, Mother Brooks embraces young David and says:

Mother Brooks
God is going to use you!

After leaving the church, on their way home not much is said between them, but the air of anxious anticipation is so thick you could cut it with a knife. Mother Brooks is beaming and David can hardly sit still. Soon they arrive. The car pulls into the driveway.

Mother Brooks says:

Mother Brooks
Here's your new home, David. This is where you are going to live.

David's mouth drops wide open. He never dreamed he'd live in such a nice home:

David
I love this house and I love you too, Mother Brooks.

Henry F. Butler, Jr.

Mother Brooks
Awe, isn't that sweet. I love you too, baby. Now let's get your things and go inside so you can see your room.

David is so excited he could jump out of his shoes!

David
Yes ma'am!

All of David's belongings are in one plastic bag, which David anxiously grabs. Mother Brooks and David enter the house and head straight for his new room. Smiling from ear-to-ear, Mother Brooks says:

Mother Brooks
Here is your room. Now tell me, what is your favorite color?

David responds with excitement:

David
Blue! My favorite color is blue.

Mother Brooks
Then blue it is! We'll paint your room blue. Alright! But first I'm going to fix you something to eat. Are you hungry?

David
Yes ma'am!

Mother Brooks
I got up early this morning and prayed, and

The Making of a Prophet

after I prayed, I made some homemade chicken gumbo soup. So all I have to do now is warm it up for you.

David
That's my favorite. Homemade chicken gumbo.

As time goes on, Mother Brooks takes David to prayer with her on a daily basis. They both have their own pillow to kneel on while they pray. One day while they are in service, the pastor calls a man to come up. The pastor anoints him with oil and the man falls to the floor under the anointing. Young David sees this, goes to the pastor, and kneels before the Lord so that the pastor can pour oil on him as well. The pastor is hesitant, but then he begins to pour oil over him. David then falls to the floor under the power of the Holy Ghost and God begins to deal with young David in visions and in revelations.

A week later while young David was in bed sleeping, he began to dream. In the dream Mother Brooks said to him:

Mother Brooks
(Dream)
I hear the sound of the garbage truck outside. Quickly young David, take this bag of garbage out for me before the truck leaves.

Young David then grabbed the garbage bag, ran to the door and took it outside. Oddly, there was a woman who was handling the garbage. And when the garbage lady saw young David, she said to him:

Garbage Lady
I'll get that garbage.

So young David handed the lady the garbage bag. But the garbage lady just set the garbage bag down on the ground, picked up young David, threw him into the back of the garbage truck, then pulled the lever for the packer to come down. Young David woke up out of his sleep crying out and trembling. Mother Brooks comes running to the room and says to young David:

Mother Brooks
What's wrong? Are you alright?"

Young David replies to her:

David
I started to have those dreams again.

She then says to young David:

Mother Brooks
When did you start having these dreams, young David?

He replies to Mother Brooks:

David
At the other house, but the people took me back to the group home 'cause of my bad dreams. Are you going to take me back too?

Mother Brooks
I'll never take you back. I promise, I'll never throw you away. We're going to make it through this, young David. We're going to make it through. You just lie back down. You'll see, everything

The Making of a Prophet

is going to be alright.

Soon after young David lies back down, he is sound asleep. Mother Brooks makes a pallet on the floor beside young David's bed and prays to the Lord all night. When morning arrives David wakes up and sees Mother Brooks lying on the floor on a pallet beside his bed:

David
I stopped having those dreams!

Mother Brooks raises up from the floor and embraces young David and says to him:

Mother Brooks
The Lord has blessed, and I am glad.

Chapter Two

The Big Day

The big day finally came when Mother Brooks received good news in the mail. Her foster care license allowing her to keep young David has arrived. Hearing a knock on the door, Mother Brooks anxiously opens it and there stands Jerry, the mailman, holding an envelope in his hand and wearing a big smile. Jerry says:

Jerry
Good morning, Mother Brooks.

Mother Brooks replies:

Mother Brooks
Good morning, Jerry. How are you doing today?

Jerry
Just fine. Mother Brooks, you told me to keep an eye

out for your letter from the state. Well, it finally came and here it is.

Mother Brooks
Thank you, Jerry.

Jerry
You're welcome, Mother Brooks. I have to be going now, but you have a nice day.

Mother Brooks
You have a nice day too, Jerry, and may the Lord bless you for what you have done.

Jerry smiles, and as he leaves he says:

Jerry
Thanks, Mother Brooks.

Mother Brooks closes her door back up and says to young David:

Mother Brooks
Young David, my foster parent license has come so that I can keep you.

Young David gives Mother Brooks a big hug and replies:

David
Alright!

Henry F. Butler, Jr.

Mother Brooks
Get your hat and coat on. We're going to drive over to the group home and show it to Deacon Murray.

David
Yes ma'am.

Then he runs into his room and gets his hat and coat. Young David comes back out and says to Mother Brooks:

David
I'm ready.

Mother Brooks puts her coat and hat on, then says to young David:

Mother Brooks
David, let's go.

They leave out of the house, get into the car and drive away. Ms. Stills sees them when they come in. She says to Mother Brooks and young David:

Ms. Stills
Good morning. How are you doing today, Mother Brooks and young David?

Mother Brooks
Fine. We're just doing fine.

David
We're doing good. We got our papers.

Ms. Stills
You got your papers?

The Making of a Prophet

Mother Brooks
Oh yes, we got them today.

Mother Brooks
Thank you Ms. Stills.

Ms. Stills rushes into Mr. Murray's office and says to him:

Ms. Stills
Mother Brooks and young David are here to see you.

Mr. Murray comes out of his office with Ms. Stills, goes over to Mother Brooks and David, and greets them both saying:

Mr. Murray
It's good to see you Mother Brooks. I want to let you know you have been doing an excellent job as a supervisor.

Mother Brooks
Thank you, Deacon Murray.

Mr. Murray
Ms. Stills said that you wanted to see me.

Mother Brooks is surprised and asks:

Mother Brooks
You didn't tell him?

Ms. Stills replies:

Henry F. Butler, Jr.

Ms. Stills
No, Mother Brooks. I thought that you would want to be the first.

Mother Brooks
You thought right. Thank you, Ms. Stills.

Mother Brooks then happily informs Mr. Murray:

Mother Brooks
Deacon Murray, my foster parent license came in the mail today and here it is.

This is welcome news for Deacon Murray, who then replies:

Mr. Murray
Alright, Mother Brooks! Alright! Now tell me, who do you want to take your place as supervisor?

Mother Brooks
You know my choice without a doubt is Ms. Stills.

Mother Brooks' unexpected choice takes Ms. Stills by surprise, and she begins to weep, responding to Mother Brooks' kindness by saying:

Ms. Stills
After what I had put you through, you still show me this kindness. From the bottom of my heart I say thank you, Mother Brooks. Thank you.

Mother Brooks
You are going to do well as the supervisor, Ms. Stills. And God has wonderful things in store for you in this new position.

Mother Brooks then gives Ms. Stills a hug. Ms. Stills can't hold back the tears.

Ms. Stills
Thanks for having so much confidence in me.

Mother Brooks says to both Deacon Murray and Ms. Stills:

Mother Brooks
Young David and I have to be going now, so may both of you have a blessed day.

Mr. Murray and Ms. Stills
You have a blessed day, Mother Brooks. You too, David.

After Mother Brooks and young David leave the building, they get into their vehicle and drive off rejoicing and praising God.

Henry F. Butler, Jr.

The Beginning of the Mission
(Elementary School)

When young David reaches school age, Mother Brooks takes him to elementary school to be enrolled. But, as time goes by, school turns out to be a challenge for young David. One day on the way home from school, one of the boys begins to tease young David about being taken out of the trash. The young boy taunts David shouting:

Tony
Trash boy! Trash boy! You were taken out of the trash!

David
I was not taken out of the trash. It's not so. It's not so.

Tony
It is so. I heard my parents talking about when you were taken out of the trash from the back of a garbage truck.

David
It's not so. It's not so. I was not taken out of the trash!

Tony
It is so. I heard my parents talking.

David ran home to where Mother Brooks was. He cried out to her saying:

The Making of a Prophet

David
It's not so! It's not so! Tell me it's not so. Tell me I wasn't taken out of the trash. It's not so. It's not so!

But Mother Brooks has a look upon her face that says different. Young David runs into his room, closes the door, falls down to his knees and begins to weep for the hurt that he feels. Mother Brooks lifts her hands up to the Lord and says:

Mother Brooks
Lord, I don't know what to do. I don't know what to say. Help him, Lord.

It's a sunshiny day with no sight of rain clouds, and all of a sudden, God makes the rain begin to pour down. Young David looks out the window at the torrential downpour. So God comforts young David through the rain, for David perceives that God's hurt is greater than his own. After God sees that young David is comforted by the rain, God stops the rain and brings forth the sun to shine. Then God gives young David a vision. In the vision, young David sees the child who has been teasing him walking on rocks and there is water all around him. David even sees himself in the vision. The boy who is walking on the rocks trips, falls down onto the rocks and cuts himself. Then he goes tumbling down into the water. There are sharks beginning to circle around the child because he is bleeding. David begins to weep about what is happening with the child. God tells David to pray:

Voice of God
Pray that I put breath back into his body and save him.

David begins to pray to the Lord:

Henry F. Butler, Jr.

David
Lord, I pray that you put
breath back into his body
and save him.

Then suddenly, God breathes the breath through the water into the child, and he stops in motion in the water. God breathes the breath through the water into the child again and he goes up out of the water. When David sees him again, he's on dry land, kneeling before the Lord with his hands lifted up.

At the same time that David is having this vision, the parents of the child are hearing how their son had been teasing young David about being taken out the trash and they confront him about it. Then they take him over to Mother Brooks' house to apologize personally. Because it is a sunshiny day with no sign of a rain cloud, they decide to walk. They make it over to Mother Brooks' and knock on her door. Mother Brooks comes to open the door. The child and his parents are standing outside the door, dripping wet. They say to Mother Brooks:

The Parents
We don't know where the
rain came from. All of a
sudden, it just came down
on us and then it stopped.

Mother Brooks
Come on in. I'll get you
some towels to dry off
with.

She calls for young David to come out of his room. Young David opens his bedroom door and comes out. He sees the child that had been teasing him and he runs over to him and embraces him. Then young David asks the boy:

David
Are you alright?

The Making of a Prophet

The child doesn't know what to think when David asks that, but he simply replies:

Tony
Yeah.

The Parents
Don't you have something to tell David?

Tony
David, I'm sorry about what I said.

David
It's okay. I am sorry too. Do you want to see my car set that my pastor gave me?

Tony
Can I?

The Parents
Go ahead, but don't get into anything.

David then takes the boy into his room to check out his car set. Tony looks at the car set and is amazed, for the car set consists of seven cars ranging from a Mustang to a Dodge Charger. All the doors open up and the steering wheels turn the front wheels. The only thing that Tony could say when he saw the cars was:

Tony
Wow!

Tony's parents say to Mother Brooks:

Henry F. Butler, Jr.

The Parents
We'll have to be going now. But it was nice to see you and David.

Mother Brooks
It was so good for both you and your son Tony to come by, and I thank you for what you have done.

Then Mother Brooks calls for David and Tony to come out of the room. They tell one another goodbye, then Tony and his parents leave.

A week later while David and the other children are at school playing on the playground, some dogs get onto the playground through an opening in the fence that surrounds the playground. The dogs see the children playing and they begin to chase the children. The children begin to run from the dogs, and the child, Tony, who had been teasing young David, trips and falls down. The dogs begin to run toward him. Young David glances back at the dogs. While he's yet running, he sees that Tony has fallen and the dogs are running towards him. David says:

David
Oh Lord!

God gives David a vision. In the vision he sees himself going against Goliath. Then young David stops and turns around. Young David looks at the dogs and says:

David
I command you to go away now in the name of Jesus. Go now, in Jesus' name!

Then David starts running toward the dogs. The dogs take off, trying to get back to the hole in the fence. The dogs go back through the hole and they leave from where the children are. Young David goes to Tony, the child who had fallen, to see if he is all right. Some of the children there begin to tease young David again about how he was taken out of the trash and they say to him:

> **Children**
> Trash boy! Trash boy!

But Tony, the child who has fallen, shouts to the other children who are teasing young David:

> **Tony**
> You mess with him, you mess with me.

So the children stop teasing young David.

Some years have passed, and David is now a young teenager. One day he comes home and finds that Mother Brooks has had a heart attack. She is doubled over in her chair and is barely conscious. David runs over to Mother Brooks and begins shaking her and pleading with her saying:

> **David**
> Don't leave me, please don't leave me.

David picks up the phone and dials 911. However, several minutes pass but the ambulance has not responded. David is desperately concerned and again cries:

> **David**
> Don't leave me, please don't leave me.

God gives David a vision. In the vision he sees his pastor preaching and his pastor says:

> **Pastor**
> God is not moved by feelings. God is moved by faith.

David then rubs his hand across his eyes to wipe away the tears. He runs into Mother Brooks' bedroom and gets her Bible. Mother Brooks had her Bible turned to the 23rd Psalm. He lifts his hands up to the Lord and begins to pray. He's praying and praying. Suddenly Mother Brooks starts breathing. She says:

Mother Brooks
AHHH!

She opens her eyes and looks over at David, who is wearing blue jeans and a T-shirt. The T-shirt is soaked with sweat from his intense prayer. David prayed through until God delivered Mother Brooks as He promised.

Mother Brooks
Come here David.

David walks over to Mother Brooks. Mother Brooks begins to talk about the plans that God has for David's life. She says:

Mother Brooks
God is going to use you mightily one day to turn the hearts of the people back unto the Lord. Just keep yourself pure before God and He will bless you.

David
I will.

Mother Brooks smiles at David and says:

Mother Brooks
Give me a hug David.

David joyfully returns the smile and gives Mother Brooks a hug.

The Making of a Prophet

David Visits the Prison

Some time has passed. David has gotten older. He and some other members of his church visit a prison facility to talk to some of the inmates. David sees three brothers standing near him and he says to them:

David
The Lord sticks closer than any brother.

Inmate #1
What do you know about being lonely?

Inmate #2
What can you tell us about being lonely? You see, our father left us when we were small. If he was standing before us now, we wouldn't even know him. We had to make it any way we could just to survive. You see, it's just a joke, it's just a big joke. You are free to come and go as you please and you say to us, "the Lord sticks closer than any brother." You probably never had a lonely day in your life. By the way you look and talk, I would say your father is probably a preacher, your mother is a teacher, you probably have a lot of brothers and sisters and a lot of cash.

Inmate #3
Man, you just spinning your wheels and talking trash. You can go now. You've done your good deed for today. I can spot a fake a mile away. You don't really know what it feels like to be lonely. You can talk it, but can you walk it? You don't know how it feels to be rejected. You've never been through that have you?

The three brothers turn and begin to walk away from David. David says to them:

David
When I was born, I was thrown away in a trash container. I then was unknowingly thrown into a garbage truck. Then I was taken out of the back of the garbage truck. So let me tell you something, I don't even know my father or my mother. I don't have any brothers or sisters. Neither do I have a lot of cash. But what I do have is Jesus and he's more than enough.

The three brothers turn back around to David. One of the three brothers says to David:

Inmate #1
Man, we are sorry for what we said. We did not know your story. Tell us about this Jesus. We'll listen to you.

David
Jesus is God's only begotten Son. He was born of a virgin, lived a sinless life, died for our sins and God raised Him from the dead on the third day. God has given us eternal life through His name. Do you believe that Jesus is the Son of God?

Inmates
We believe that Jesus is the Son of God.

So they give their lives to the Lord and David goes on to say to the three brothers:

David
Now say, "I denounce anything that is unholy, anything that is not like God. I denounce it now, in Jesus' name."

The three brothers say to The Lord:

Inmates
I denounce everything that is unholy, everything that's not like God. I denounce it now, in Jesus' name.

David
Now say, "I forgive everyone who's ever hurt me, done me wrong, or spoken negativity into my life."

The three brothers are slow at saying they forgive. David says to the three brothers:

David
If you do not forgive, God will not forgive you.

Inmates
I forgive anyone who has ever hurt me, done me wrong or spoken negativity into my life.

David
I forgive myself, that Satan may not bring me into condemnation over past sins that God has already forgiven me for.

Inmates
I forgive myself, that Satan may not bring me into condemnation over past sins that God has already forgiven me for.

David looks at the three brothers and he sees that their appearance has changed. David then says:

The Making of a Prophet

David
You should bow on your knees before the Lord, because he is the King of glory.

The three brothers defiantly respond:

Inmates
We don't go down on our knees for nobody.

David waits for a little while longer, then he tells the three brothers:

David
I have to be going now, but the Lord will surely bring you out from this place. Just don't forget the Lord after He brings you out.

Inmate #1
Man it's no time to be telling jokes. You know what we are in here for? Armed robbery. We are looking at 30 years and you say that God is going to bring us out.

David
Just don't forget him when He brings you out.

David gives them one of the church bibles and then he leaves with the other church members that he came with.

Chapter Three

The Mission

As the years progress, David graduates from high school. The pastor buys David a car and Mother Brooks buys David a coat for his graduation. David is excited. Pastor Bowen shows David a bag and places it in the trunk of the car. Then he says to David:

> **Pastor**
> One day you're going to be
> needing this.

With all the excitement, David forgets about the bag in the trunk. They have prayer that night but David doesn't make it because he is out celebrating his graduation. As David pulls into the church parking lot, he spots a man going around to the back of the church. David gets out of his car and walks around to the back of the church. He looks around and sees the man digging through the trash in the church dumpster. David says to the man:

The Making of a Prophet

David
Mister, what are you looking for?

The man replies:

Bum
I'm lookin' for my treasure.

David replies:

David
The true treasure is in the inside and not on the outside.

The man says to David:

Bum
I know, but I traded my family watch, the only thing that I had left of value, for this treasure map. These two young men told me I would find gold and diamonds. I asked them, "you wouldn't lie to an old man would you?" And they said, "noooooo." So I traded my watch for this treasure map and the map led me to this dumpster. It has to be here. It just has to. So I'm going to keep on lookin' until one day I find my treasure.

David says to the man:

David
I pray one day you find what you are looking for.

The man says to David:

Bum
When I find it, I'm going to come to your service.

David leaves the man and goes inside the church. The pastor looks around, and here comes David walking in. Pastor John says to David:

Pastor
For a moment I didn't think that you were going to make it.

David
Nothing can keep me from praying.

David falls on his knees and begins to worship the Lord saying:

David
Lord, I praise and I worship you, for you are the great and awesome God. For you have declared in your word: "Behold, I am the Lord, the God of all flesh: is there anything too hard for me?" For truly Lord, I know that nothing is too hard for you, so Lord, I pray that one day I might be able to see my father and my mother. In Jesus' name, amen.

The Making of a Prophet

Mother Brooks hears what David prays and begins to cry.

Years have passed and David is now about twenty years old. One day when Pastor John and his wife Elisabeth are home having breakfast, she says:

> **First Lady**
> Pastor John, I've been dreaming the same dream for the last few nights. I dreamed that there was going to be an unusual wedding in our church.

She goes on to describe things in the new church, even though she isn't able to see the church because she went blind before they moved into the new church. Pastor John waves his hand in front of her face to confirm that she still can't see. After doing so, he just has a look of amazement on his face.

One day David goes out to the field, as he would often do, to meditate and to pray. There is a guy named Billy and his girlfriend Janet out in the field. Billy's father is a police officer who is up for promotion to be a sergeant. Janet's father is the mayor of the city. He is speaking at a community gathering nearby. Billy's and Janet's fathers are best friends who had grown up together. Both Billy's and Janet's mothers are deceased. Billy has one of his father's guns. He's playing with the gun near his girlfriend, and it accidentally goes off and fatally injures her. David goes over to where Billy is and says:

> **David**
> Billy, I saw what happened. It was an accident. I saw it.

Billy gets nervous. As he is shaking, he tosses the gun over to David. The people start to gather around to see what is going on. They see David with the gun and the girl lying lifeless on the ground. One of the men out of the crowd runs over to her and kneels down on one knee. It's Mayor Wilson, who says to her:

Mayor
Janet, can you hear me?
Can you hear me, Janet?

But Janet doesn't respond. He then checks her pulse, looks up and says:

Mayor
She's dead! Janet is dead!

He then looks over at David holding the gun and shouts:

Mayor
You killed her!

David
No way! I didn't kill her!

Mayor
You killed my daughter and I'm going to get you for this!

Billy, the guy who did the actual killing, also accuses David saying:

Billy
You killed her. You killed Janet!

David exclaims:

David
No! No!

The mayor is overcome with anger and he screams at David:

The Making of a Prophet

Mayor
I'm going to get you for what you've done to my daughter. I'm going to get you!

He begins to run with the crowd chasing David, who cries out:

David
No, no, no!

David runs through a nearby wooded area and loses them. The crowd gives up on catching David and they turn back from chasing him. Then Janet's father drops down to his knees and weeps bitterly, crying out:

Mayor
Janet, my baby. My little girl is gone.

In grief, his head drops as he continues to cry. Suddenly the police arrive on the scene. The officer begins to ask the bystanders:

Police
Did anyone see who murdered the girl?

One person from the crowd shouts:

Bystander
Yeah, he ran.

The police asks:

Police
Does anyone know his name?

A person from the crowd answers:

Henry F. Butler, Jr.

Person
David Bowen. He lives with Mother Brooks.

The police go to Mother Brooks home. They knock on the door. Mother Brooks answers and opens the door. One police officer asks:

Police
May we come inside ma'am? We have a few questions to ask you.

Mother Brooks
Yes. Come on in.

The police officers enter her house. One of the police officers asks:

Police
Where's David?

Mother Brooks
Why, is anything wrong?

Police
When was the last time you saw David?

Mother Brooks
Tell me, is there anything wrong?

Police
David is wanted for the murder of Janet Wilson and we've come to arrest him.

The Making of a Prophet

Mother Brooks
No, no! I don't believe it. David didn't kill Janet. David wouldn't kill nobody. You're looking for the wrong person. There must be some kind of mistake. David didn't kill her!

Mother Brooks begins to break down and cry. The police officer responds to Mother Brooks, saying:

Police
When David comes home, could you please tell him to turn himself in. It will go better for him if he did that.

Mother Brooks
David didn't do it officers! David didn't do it!

The police officers leave Mother Brooks' residence and drive away. Mother Brooks is devastated and cries out to the Lord:

Mother Brooks
Lord, this isn't true. This isn't true, Lord. Lord, help David. Help him, Lord, in Jesus' name.

She then gets on the phone and calls the pastor. Mother Brooks says:

Henry F. Butler, Jr.

Mother Brooks
The police came to the house a little while ago and they say that David is wanted for murder. They say that he killed Janet Wilson. But I don't believe it, Pastor John. You know David wouldn't kill nobody. Something is wrong here Pastor. Someone is trying to frame David!

Pastor
I don't believe it either. I'm going to go before the Lord about this. Don't you even worry. The Lord is going to protect and deliver David from all harm and danger.

Mother Brooks
Thank you, Pastor.

Pastor
Just don't worry. It's in the Lord's hand now.

Mother Brooks
Alright Pastor, goodbye.

Then she hangs up the phone. Meanwhile, Billy, the guy who killed his girlfriend, tells his father what had happened. His father, Officer Joey, gets upset about what his son did. He not only killed someone, but he killed Joey's best friend's daughter. How could Joey ever stand to look the mayor in his face if the mayor knew that it was his son, Tony, who killed his daughter Janet? She was all the mayor had left because his wife had passed away a few years ago and he was raising Janet by himself. Officer Joey tells Tony:

Officer Joey
Keep quiet. I'll take care of this.

Officer Joey then goes out into a field, takes out his gun and shoots himself in the arm in such a way that the bullet would only graze him. He wants it to appear as though David has lost his mind and has even shot a police officer. David sees what's going on from where he is hiding in the field. He makes it to where he parked his car, gets in and drives away. David drives and drives. David stops the car, gets out and begins to walk. David walks under the bridge, sees a homeless man lying on the ground, wine bottle at his side, trembling from the cold. David takes off his coat that Mother Brooks had given him, and lays it over the homeless man and walks away. The homeless man slightly raises up with one eye open, then he falls back down to the ground. David walks back to his car, gets in and drives off.

David keeps driving until his car suddenly stops. David tries to start his car again, but it won't start. Soon, the car windows begin to frost up because of the cold. Eventually, the police officers who have been searching for David come to the place where David's car has stopped, and after spotting him, they order him to step out of the car with his hands up. But David is determined not to move – he's not getting out – for he perceives by the Spirit of God that danger lies ahead. It's cold outside and he starts to tremble and begins to cry. He tries to lift his hands up to the Lord, so he raises his hands just a little bit. Then he slowly inches them up a little higher as he begins to slump down in his seat.

The homeless man who's under the bridge raises up again and says to the Lord:

Homeless Man
I know we haven't talked in a long time, but I'm not praying on behalf of myself. I'm praying for the one who has shown me this kindness in my hour of distress. No matter what situation he

may find himself in, Lord
I pray that you cover him
with your warmth. Do this
for me, Lord. Do this for
me. In Jesus' name, do this
for me.

Then he falls back down to the ground. Suddenly there is a fog that covers David's car and water begins to drip from his car. The car is not running, but God is defrosting his car. A circle begins to form on David's windshield. The circle gets bigger and bigger. God gives David a vision of when he was younger. Mother Brooks has David on the altar, calling on the name of Jesus. In the vision, Mother Brooks says to David:

Mother Brooks
Say, "Jesus."

David says lightly out loud:

David
Jesus.

In the vision Mother Brooks says to David:

Mother Brooks
Say it like you mean it.

David says it again:

David
JESUS!

Every time David would say Jesus, he would get a little stronger. God gives David another vision. This time his pastor is walking toward him with his arm extended out and his finger pointing toward David. He's saying the twenty-third Psalm.

Pastor
The Lord is my shepherd; I shall not want. He maketh me to lie down in green pastures: he leadeth me beside the still waters. He restoreth my soul: he leadeth me in the paths of righteousness for his name's sake. Yea, though I walk through the valley of the shadow of death, I will fear no evil: for thou art with me.

When Pastor John gets to the verse that says, *"I will fear no evil: for thou art with me",* David shakes himself.

God then stirs the three brothers who David had witnessed to at the prison. David's name came up and the three brothers said to each other:

Inmates
God must want us to pray for David.

So they pray for David. Inexplicably, there are hands coming together around David's car like electricity. God then stirs up Mother Brooks and she gets out of bed, gets down on her knees and speaks out to the Lord:

Mother Brooks
Thy servant heareth thee, oh Lord.

She then begins to pray for David and there were more hands coming together around David's car like electricity. God then stirs up Pastor John and he calls Sister Wade, the church secretary. Sister Wade is wearing a robe and has curlers in her hair. When she answers the phone, Pastor John says:

Henry F. Butler, Jr.

Pastor
God has called for a shut-in.

Sister Wade
When, Pastor?

Pastor
Now.

Sister Wade
All right, Pastor.

Pastor John tells Sister Wade to call up the members of the congregation and ask them to gather at the church to pray for David. Sister Wade calls the members up and they start making their way to the house of the Lord.

God stirs up another church and they begin to pray for David also. More hands start going around David's car just like electricity, the hands start going around David's car. The pastor and the members have made it to the church. They begin to position themselves for prayer. God stirs up Pastor John and he cries out:

Pastor
Lord, send warring angels.
Protect David from all
harm and danger.

Suddenly, angels start to appear around David's car. One in the front, one in the back, one on the left and one on the right. They have swords in their hands, raised up and ready for battle. So many angels start appearing that the police who had been surrounding David are now the ones who are surrounded. David keeps on saying:

David
JESUS!

As David calls out the name of Jesus, he gets stronger and stronger.

The Making of a Prophet

Then two of the warring angels nod one to the other, and suddenly the sound of a rushing mighty wind is heard, and a swirling ring of fire appears that encircles the car with a barrier that cannot be breached. Then above the angels the heavens open up, the clouds roll away like a scroll, and a great fireball falls from heaven that penetrates the car and strikes David in the chest. Immediately David's hands go up and his body is aglow from the glorious heavenly flame. David lays his hand on the steering wheel of his car and begins to pray:

David
Father in the name of Jesus, let this car start back up.

David then turns the ignition on and the car starts.

David
Thank you, Lord. Thank you, Lord. Thank you. Thank you, Jesus.

God stirs up Mother Brooks in prayer and she also prays:

Mother Brooks
Lord I pray that you stir up the one who really did the killing. Don't let him rest day or night until deliverance has come forth, and Lord bring David home. Bring him home, Lord. Bring David home, in Jesus' name.

Henry F. Butler, Jr.

Confessions

The Lord gives Billy a dream. He dreams he's in a dry deserted place. It is dark and dimly lit. He starts hearing someone crying as if they were mourning. He makes his way over to where the noise is coming from. It comes from a mysterious opening in the earth. He lies down on the ground and cautiously peeps in. The hole is like a dark bottomless pit. People are crying out in agony; they are suffering and in pain. It is like an elevator going down and voices are crying out:

Voices
Help me, Lord. I'll treat everyone right. I will do right.
I'll forgive. Just help me.

There's nothing down there but darkness, thick darkness. Billy then sees himself down there in hell. He wakes up and starts to tremble and screams out:

Billy
No. No. No. No!

He opens the door of the house and runs out into the street, terrified and trembling. A police officer who sees Billy running through the traffic recognizes who he is. He turns to his partner and says:

Officer Tim
That's Officer Joey's son.

They catch up with him and tell him to get into the car. Billy gets in the car. They take him to the police station, where Billy confesses:

The Making of a Prophet

Billy
I am the one who killed Janet Wilson! My father told me to keep quiet about what happened!

Captain
What?

Then the captain tells the other police officers:

Captain
Come on, let's get over there where they have David!

They race their way to David's location, lights flashing and sirens blaring away. Meanwhile, David puts his car in gear and begins to drive away. The policemen trying to apprehend David have their weapons pointed at him and are ready to fire, but they can't do anything because God has them surrounded. David just drives off. The captain and his officers suddenly arrive where the other officers had just had David surrounded.

The captain and the officers with him exit their squads and immediately go over to Officer Joey to confront him. Officer Joey doesn't know why the captain is there:

Officer Joey
Captain, what brings you out here?

Captain
Hand over your weapons.

The other officers with the captain point their weapons at Officer Joey. Officer Joey offers no resistance and hands over his weapons. After the captain reads Joey his rights he says:

Captain
Joey, you're under arrest for obstructing justice and withholding evidence in the murder of Janet Wilson.

Joey gets into the car. They take him down to the police station and book him. Meanwhile, David just drives aimlessly. He looks down at his gas gauge and there's less than an eighth of a tank left. David is dirty, hungry and thirsty. He spots a restaurant up the road on the right hand side, but his money is spent. He decides just to go in and clean himself up, and perhaps he'll get a glass of water to drink to quench his thirst.

David pulls into the restaurant parking lot and parks his car. When he parks his car, the trunk of his car opens up. David gets out of his car to close the trunk. When he goes around to the back of the car he sees the bag that his pastor had placed in his trunk after he had given him this car for his graduation.

Amazingly, two years have passed and the bag is still in David's trunk untouched. David opens the bag and finds a washcloth, a bar of soap, a razor and a change of clothes. David says:

David
Thank you Lord, thank you.

He goes into the restaurant and asks the maître d:

David
Where's your bathroom?

The maître d directs David to the bathroom. David takes the bag, goes to the bathroom and washes up and shaves. He changes clothes. Then David lifts his hands up and begins to thank the Lord for his goodness and His mercy. David reaches into his pocket and there's money in his pocket too. His pastor had put fifty dollars in his pocket for him. Now David has plenty of money for his meal:

David
Thank you, Lord. Thank you, Lord for making a way for me.

After David finishes his meal, he leaves the restaurant, stops to get some gas, then begins the long drive back home. David drives and drives into the dark distance.

Chapter Four

The Blessings

The pimp and his girlfriend are inside their house. Tensions between them are brewing. God then begins to move on the young lady's heart. Feeling the conviction of the Lord, she approaches the pimp and says:

Girlfriend
I am going to church. I am tired of living in sin. I am going back to church. You gave me a ring, we got a marriage license, and we still haven't gotten married. I want to get my life right with the Lord. I am tired of being a backslider.

He tries to hold her back and says to her:

The Making of a Prophet

Pimp
Baby, you know that I love you.

His girlfriend responds:

Girlfriend
If you love me so much like you say that you do, then why haven't we gotten married?

The pimp is silent. He doesn't have a response to her inquiry. More determined now, she says:

Girlfriend
I'm going to church.

She breaks loose from him. She puts her wedding ring and the marriage license into her purse. She suddenly opens the door and flees, running desperately towards the church. Some police cars approach the house, lights flashing and sirens sounding as they respond to some other emergency. The pimp gets nervous when he hears the police cars, slips out of the house and also heads toward the church. When the pimp and his girlfriend enter the church, they don't recognize it, because the former pastor and congregation have moved to a new church across town, and a new congregation is now in this church.

Sister Molly, who is kneeling and praying, raises up from her prayer position and sees the pimp and his girlfriend coming into the church. She goes over to where they are. She greets both of them by saying:

Sis. Molly
I'm so glad both of you have come.

After looking at the young lady who has entered the church, she suddenly recognizes her and says:

Henry F. Butler, Jr.

Sis. Molly
Donna Brooks…Is that you? I haven't seen you in about twenty two years. You just had turned twenty when I last saw you. Remember how I used to let you play nurse when you were a child? You were really good at it. I even thought that one day you would become a nurse. But that was then, this is now. By the way, has your mother seen you since you've been back?

Donna responds to Sis. Molly:

Donna
No, not yet.

Sis. Molly says:

Sis. Molly
Donna, I know that she will be glad to see you.

Josh, another member of the congregation, raises up and sees Sis. Molly talking to Donna and the pimp. He then gets up off of his knees and walks back to where they are. Josh looks at the man and says:

Josh
Don't I know you? You're Daniel Bowen, Pastor John Bowen's son.

Both Daniel Bowen, who is the pimp, and Donna, are in a state of shock. Out of all the churches they chose to step foot in, they picked their

The Making of a Prophet

parents' new church; a congregation they had been away from all these years. But all this is unsettling to Daniel:

> **Daniel**
> Yeah, but we really have to be going now.

But Josh responds saying:

> **Josh**
> Man it's so good to see you again. Last time I saw you, you told me you where involved in some type of business deal. By the way you look and dress, it seems like you've done well for yourself. Are those really alligator shoes you got on? Suede hat, coat, diamond watch and ring, gold chain on your neck. By the way, what did you say you do for a living?

Daniel is really getting uncomfortable with Josh's probing questions:

> **Daniel**
> We really have to be going.

Donna agrees, saying:

> **Donna**
> We really do have to be going.

Daniel says to Josh:

Henry F. Butler, Jr.

> **Daniel**
> Tell dad and mom I'm sorry that we couldn't stay long. We gotta be going now.

Right at that moment, Pastor John raises up and turns around and sees Josh and Sister Molly talking to two people who had come into the church. He gets up to go welcome them. Daniel sees his father getting up. He takes a handkerchief out and wipes his forehead. Daniel says:

> **Daniel**
> Oh, Lord.

Pastor John looks, and he's shocked – there's his long lost son. Daniel has finally returned. Pastor John says:

> **Pastor**
> Daniel, you have come home, son. I didn't give up on you. I knew one day you would return.

When Pastor John calls out Daniel's name, everybody rises up and turns around. First Lady says:

> **First Lady**
> Daniel, is that really you son?

She gets up and starts feeling her way to Daniel. Daniel asks his father:

> **Daniel**
> What happened to mom's eyesight?

Pastor John replies:

The Making of a Prophet

Pastor
When you left home, your mother lost her sight.

Daniel immediately breaks down and cries, for his heart yearns for his mother to be able to see him once again. Daniel always loved his mother. From that news, Daniel begins to blame himself. He thought, "how could I ever do something that would cause her harm?" While Daniel is in the midst of his contrition, Pastor John says to Daniel:

Pastor
We don't break down here, we pray. You know what you must do.

Daniel says to the First Lady:

Daniel
Here I come, mom.

He goes to his mother and says:

Daniel
Mom.

His mother replies:

First Lady
Daniel, is that really you? You've come home. The Lord has answered my prayer.

Daniel and his mother embrace. Mother Brooks is there rejoicing about Daniel coming home. She looks up, sees her daughter standing and says:

Mother Brooks
Donna, is that you?

Donna excitedly responds:

Donna
Mama!

She runs to her mother and they engage in a passionate embrace. Mother Brooks kisses her on the forehead and says:

Mother Brooks
Baby, I've been praying for you.

As a spirit of loving reconciliation permeates the room, tears of joy begin to flow. Pastor John says:

Pastor
Daniel and Donna. We gladly say to the both of you, welcome home.

Saints
Welcome home.

Daniel and Donna respond to this loving welcome back by saying:

Daniel and Donna
We want to rededicate our lives to Jesus.

So they give their lives back to the Lord. Pastor Bowen says:

Pastor
This has been a good day. A very good day for us. But we can't forget why we're here. Everybody back down on our knees and pray for David.

The Making of a Prophet

So everyone goes back down on their knees. As they go into intercession for David, the homeless man who was lying on the ground under the bridge raises up again. He gets up from the ground and throws his wine bottle down. He then says:

> **Homeless Man**
> I'm going home.

He starts making his way to the house of the Lord. He makes it to the church and goes inside. Some of the members speak about the way he's dressed. The homeless man lowers his head down. Pastor John shouts:

> **Pastor**
> "No! Don't do that! This is Prophet Elijah Green. A mighty man of God!

The homeless man raises his head. Pastor John goes on to say:

> **Pastor**
> Twenty-five years ago, he was out on a crusade evangelizing. When he returned home, he learned that his family had been burned up in a fire. He left the church after that happened and hadn't been seen until now. But now he has come home!

Then Pastor John embraces him and says:

> **Pastor**
> Welcome home, Prophet Elijah Green. Welcome home.

Pastor John then says to the congregation:

Henry F. Butler, Jr.

Pastor
You don't know who God has your miracle tied to.

Members of the congregation embrace and they all say to Prophet Green:

Saints
Welcome home.

Mother Brooks recognizes the coat that he has on and says:

Mother Brooks
That's David's coat.

It's the coat she bought him for his graduation. So she asks Prophet Green:

Mother Brooks
Have you seen him?

Prophet Green replies,

Prophet
I was cold and laying under a bridge, and he took off his coat and covered me with it.

He then asks:

Prophet
Do you want it back?

Mother Brooks replies:

The Making of a Prophet

> **Mother Brooks**
> No. He gave it to you. May the Lord turn it into a blessing for him.

Prophet Green says to Mother Brooks:

> **Prophet**
> I pray that the Lord will give David the desires of his heart.

Shortly after that, Pastor John sees Daniel while Donna, Mother Brooks' daughter, also approaches. Daniel says:

> **Daniel**
> We want to do what is right. We want to get married.

Pastor John replies:

> **Pastor**
> It's good that you both want to do what's right. But you have to have a marriage license and a wedding ring for the bride.

Daniel and Donna respond:

> **Daniel and Donna**
> We have them!

Donna takes the marriage license and the ring that Daniel had given her out of her purse. Pastor John hesitates for a moment and then says:

Henry F. Butler, Jr.

> **Pastor**
> Let's do it!

So they start getting things in the church ready for the marriage. Some of the women come up to the pastor and ask him:

> **Saints**
> Can we make a wedding dress out of the communion cloth, because what she has on is not appropriate for a wedding? The communion cloth is Holy because it's dedicated to the Lord, and Donna has given her life back to the Lord, so her body is dedicated unto the Lord.

Pastor John hesitates after the sisters explain why they want to use the communion cloth. But he finally says:

> **Pastor**
> O.K. Let's do it.

So they take Donna to one of the rooms in the church to get her ready. Daniel goes to his father and asks:

> **Daniel**
> Is there a room or a restroom I can go in for a moment?

Pastor John replies:

> **Pastor**
> You have to make it quick. You don't have long before the wedding.

The Making of a Prophet

Daniel says to his father:

Daniel
It's something I have to do first.

Pastor John shows Daniel where the restroom is and Daniel goes into the restroom and closes the door. There's a garbage chute in the restroom that goes to the dumpster outside. Daniel takes off his suede hat, suede coat and his alligator shoes and puts them into the trash. He takes off his diamond cufflinks, diamond ring, diamond watch and his gold chain and pushes all of it into the garbage chute, and they go outside to the dumpster. He then lifts his hands up to the Lord with tears streaming down his face:

Daniel
Now, Mom...Lord...Mom!

He wants so badly for the Lord to restore his mother's eyesight. Then suddenly, someone knocks on the restroom door and says:

Person
Time for the wedding to start.

Daniel comes out of the restroom wearing only his shirt and pants. His sleeves are rolled up, and he is only wearing socks on his feet. Pastor John is shocked and says:

Pastor
Son, I can't let you get married like that.

He takes off his suitcoat and his shoes and gives them to Daniel. Pastor John then says:

Henry F. Butler, Jr.

Pastor
I know it's nothing to compare with what you had on, but it's the best I have. When you were small, you used to put on my coat and shoes trying to imitate me.

Daniel embraces his father and says:

Daniel
I still do. Thanks dad.

He then takes the coat and shoes from his father and puts them on. Pastor John goes up to the podium. Daniel comes up and stands in place for the wedding. Then Donna comes in, just glowing in her wedding dress that was made from the communion cloth. She looks at Daniel as he has his father's coat and shoes on. She smiles, for she had prayed that Daniel would return back to his old self, but she didn't know it would be this quick. Pastor John goes through the vows with them. Daniel salutes his bride. Then Donna takes the bouquet and throws it over her shoulder in back of her, and the bouquet goes to where the First Lady is at the piano. Just as the bouquet starts to come down, the First Lady's eyes open and her eyesight returns to her. She catches the bouquet. Pastor John then calls her:

Pastor
Elisabeth?

Elisabeth then excitedly responds:

First Lady
I can see you, John! I can see everybody!

Pastor John makes his way back to where Elisabeth is, salutes her and says:

The Making of a Prophet

Pastor
This has definitely been a good day for us. But still we can't forget about David. So everyone back on our knees.

So they went back down on their knees in prayer for David. In the meantime, back at the police station the captain radios Officer Tim and says:

Captain
Officer Tim, what's your twenty? Over.

Officer Tim responds:

Officer Tim
I'm still in the building, captain. Over.

The captain replies:

Captain
Could you come to my office, please?"

Officer Tim responds:

Officer Tim
I'm headed that way now, sir.

Officer Tim comes into the captain's office and says:

Officer Tim
Captain, you wanted to see me?

The captain replies:

Captain
Yes I do, Officer Tim. I'd like for you to drive over to Welcome Home Church. I heard that they are there at the church having a special prayer for David. Tell them that we have in custody the one who really did the killing of Janet Wilson, and we have his father for obstruction of justice. Tell them that David has been cleared of all charges, and ask Mother Brooks if she could find it in her heart to forgive us about what we put her through concerning David. Also tell Pastor John and the rest of the members that we're sorry. Could you do that for me?

Officer Tim says to the captain:

Officer Tim
Yes Sir.

Officer Tim leaves the captain's office and exits the building. He then gets into his squad car and drives over to the church. After parking, he walks up to the church and goes inside. Pastor John and the members are still down on their knees in prayer. Officer Tim clears his throat to get their attention. Pastor John and the members rise up, turn around, and there standing behind them is Officer Tim. He's wearing a big smile. Pastor John then says to Officer Tim:

The Making of a Prophet

Pastor
By that smile that you have on your face, I take it that everything is okay.

Officer Tim says to Pastor John:

Officer Tim
Yes, pastor. The captain has sent me to tell everyone the good news.

Pastor John is anxious to know and replies:

Pastor
What good news are you speaking of Officer Tim?

Officer Tim gladly answers Pastor John:

Officer Tim
David has been cleared of all charges. We now have in custody the one who really killed Janet, and we have his father for obstruction of justice. Mother Brooks, the captain also wanted me to ask you if you could find it in your heart to forgive us about the worries we put you through concerning David.

Mother Brooks then says to Officer Tim:

Mother Brooks
You know I will.

Officer Tim continues to say:

> **Officer Tim**
> Pastor John, the captain also wanted me to tell you and the rest of the congregation that we are sorry for what we put you through as well.

Pastor John says:

> **Pastor**
> Tell your captain that we forgive him for what he did as well. Officer Tim, tell your captain it took a big man to do what he has done.

Officer Tim says:

> **Officer Tim**
> Thanks, Pastor John. I'll tell him that.

Officer Tim goes on to say to Pastor John:

> **Officer Tim**
> By the way Pastor John... Is David still going to be speaking in the Friday night service?

Pastor John replies:

The Making of a Prophet

> **Pastor**
> I pray that the Lord will bring him back in time to do so.

Officer Tim says to Pastor John:

> **Officer Tim**
> I believe that He will, Pastor John.

Pastor John says to Officer Tim:

> **Pastor**
> I believe that He will, too, Officer Tim.

Officer Tim says to Pastor John:

> **Officer Tim**
> I have to be going now, Pastor John. But you and the members have a blessed day.

Pastor John replies:

> **Pastor**
> You have a blessed day as well, Officer Tim.

Officer Tim leaves the church, gets into his squad car and drives back to the police station. Pastor John and all the members rejoice about what God has done for David. Pastor John then says to the members:

Henry F. Butler, Jr.

Pastor
I believe our work here is done. The only thing left now is for God to send David home, and I believe that He will. So members, this shut-in has officially ended.

So everyone leaves the church and goes home.

The Making of a Prophet

David Comes Home

David was tired of driving, so he pulled over to the side of the road and took a nap. While he was sleeping, God gave David a dream about going home. So he started his car back up, turned it around and headed back towards home. David makes it to the house and parks his car. He walks up to the door of the house, takes out his key and opens the door. Mother Brooks looks up from where she is sitting. She is reading her bible and there stands David in the doorway. Mother Brooks gets up from the chair and says to David:

Mother Brooks
You're home!

David runs over to Mother Brooks and engages in a tearful embrace. Then David says:

David
God gave me a dream about coming home.

Mother Brooks says:

Mother Brooks
It's so good to see you David. God has watched over you and taken good care of you. David, the police have in custody the one who really killed Janet Wilson, and they are holding his father for obstruction of justice. David, you have been cleared of all charges. Isn't God good, David?

David says:

David
Yes, he is. Truly the Lord is good. I have to go over to Pastor John's house to tell him that I'm back, and to get ready for the service tonight.

Mother Brooks says to David:

Mother Brooks
Pastor John and First Lady will be glad to see you, too. And David, God has even restored First Lady's eyesight. She sees now! David, she will be able to see you after all these years. She will be finally able to see you.

David says to Mother Brooks:

David
I can't wait to see her smiling face, her joyful heart - and now she's able to see! All I can say is...Lord, thanks. Thank you, Lord for loving us so much. Thank you, Lord. I have to be going now. I can't wait to see her myself. I know Pastor John was running and jumping all over the church!

Mother Brooks says to David:

Mother Brooks
He was. Indeed he was. And guess what David, they even Pastor and First Lady renewed their vows.

David says to Mother Brooks:

David
You know I got to go now. You are going to be at the service tonight, aren't you?"

Mother Brooks says to David:

Mother Brooks
You know that I am.

David gives Mother Brooks a hug and kisses her on her jaw. Then David says to Mother Brooks:

David
I'll see you there.

David leaves out of the house, gets back in his car and drives over to Pastor John and First Lady's house. A little after David leaves Mother Brooks' house, her daughter, Donna, comes by to visit. Mother Brooks starts talking about grandchildren. Mother Brooks says to Donna:

Mother Brooks
It's going to be good to have grandchildren around here one day to spoil.

Then Donna begins to weep and to cry out for Jesus. She cries out saying:

Henry F. Butler, Jr.

Donna
You would have had a grandson, but I threw him in the trash. I am so sorry.

Mother Brooks puts her arms around Donna to try to comfort her daughter, but Mother Brooks is hurt by what her daughter has done. Donna continues crying and shouting:

Donna
I am so sorry. I am so sorry that I threw my son in the trash can.

Then it dawns on Mother Brooks, and she remembers that David had been thrown away in the trash after he was born. Meanwhile, Donna is still distraught:

Donna
He's dead...he's dead. I put him in the trash can. I am so sorry. I am so sorry. Forgive me, Lord. Please forgive me! I am so sorry. I am so sorry, Lord!

Mother Brooks then says to Donna:

Mother Brooks
Where did you put him in the trash?

Donna says to her mother:

Donna
Does it matter? He's dead. I threw my son in the trash and he's dead. I am so sorry. Please forgive me. I threw

The Making of a Prophet

him in the trash.

Mother Brooks says again:

> **Mother Brooks**
> But where did you throw him in the trash? Where?

She tells her, and Mother Brooks says:

> **Mother Brooks**
> Lord, could this be? Could this be, Lord?

Mother Brooks realizes that the child she has raised up is indeed her very own grandson. Mother Brooks looks at her daughter and says:

> **Mother Brooks**
> He's alive! He's alive!

Mother Brooks begins to tell her daughter how he was taken out of the trash. She tells her daughter, Donna, that she has been taking care of him for the last sixteen years. He was just four years old when she had gotten custody of him. Mother Brooks says to Donna:

> **Mother Brooks**
> As a matter of fact, David will be speaking tonight at church service. Would you come with me to tonight's service?

Donna looks at her and says:

> **Donna**
> I can't! I can't!

For she was ashamed of what she had done.

Henry F. Butler, Jr.

Families Reunited

God begins to move on the three brothers that David had witnessed to in the prison, and the glory of the Lord comes upon them. They begin to praise and worship the Lord saying:

3 Inmates
Lord, we just thank you for your goodness and mercy following us all the days of our lives. We want to thank you also for your loving kindness that has drawn us to you, Lord. We rest in you. For you said there is nothing too hard for you; therefore, we cast all of our cares upon you because you care for us.

Then they fall down on their knees before the King of glory. The guard that had been giving the three brothers a hard time comes to their cells and says to them:

Guard #1
Follow me.

The three brothers are confused about what is going on. So they say to the guard:

3 Inmates
What did we do this time?

The guard just repeats himself and says to the three brothers:

Guard #1
Follow me.

The Making of a Prophet

They follow the guard as he leads them out of the jail section and takes them to the front. There at the front, they are given a change of clothes. They are told to clean themselves up and to change their clothes. The three brothers are more confused. Not only have they been taken out of their cells, but now each one of them is given a two-piece suit, shirt, tie, socks and shoes. They even receive overcoats. After they clean up and change their clothes, they are told:

Guard #1
You are free to go and there's a driver waiting outside to take you where you need to go.

One of the brothers says:

Inmate #2
Pinch me so I can see if I am awake or dreaming.

Another replies:

Inmate #1
You have to be awake, or else the three of us are dreaming the same dream.

So they leave out of the police station. Outside, the driver is waiting for them. The driver opens the door for the brothers to get in the limousine. They enter the limousine, the driver closes the door, goes around to the driver's side, gets in, turns around to them and says:

Driver
I guess you are wondering how you got from the prison to the limo. I'll tell you: God stirred up the governor in a dream. The gov-

ernor told it to everybody that would listen, so you might as well hear it too. In the dream, God told the governor not to hold his servants, the three brothers, any longer. He said, "You must let them go now, for they must come into my sanctuary to eat of the meal that I have prepared for them." The governor came running through the house trembling. Two days have passed since he dreamed that dream, and he hasn't been able to go back to sleep since then. The governor told me to get your sizes and to buy each of you a change of clothes. So this I have done. The governor also told me to ask you to pray for him that he may be able to sleep again.

The three brothers reply:

3 Brothers
We'll be glad to pray for him.

The driver then asks:

Driver
And could you pray for me too?

The Making of a Prophet

They take his hand and begin to pray for the governor and the driver. After they finish praying, the driver asks the three brothers:

> **Driver**
> Where would you like me to take you?

All the three brothers had was the address of David's church; it was embossed on the bible that David had given them. They answer:

> **3 Brothers**
> Can you take us to the address that is on this Bible?

The driver says to the three brothers:

> **Driver**
> I will be glad to take you there. I know the area.

So the driver pulls out and starts driving to the church. David is sitting in a seat on the church podium just smiling and rejoicing, glad not only because God has brought him back home, but also because God has restored First Lady Bowen's sight. Pastor and First Lady Bowen are sitting in the front row seats. Sitting with them on the front row seat is Prophet Elijah Green, Mother Brooks, Sam, Josh, Sister Molly, Sister Wade, the police captain, Officer Tim, Tony and his parents, the doctor, Deacon Murray, Ms. Stills and Jerry. They all have come out to hear the word that God has put in David.

Meanwhile, the man who had traded his family's watch for the treasure map looks back over the map again and traces his steps in case he had made a wrong turn along the way, but it still led him back to the church's garbage dumpster. The bum says to himself:

> **The Bum**
> This just has to be the right place, it just has to be.

So he decides to give it one more look, for he has come too far to give up now. He places both hands on top of the church's garbage dumpster, pulls himself up and looks in, and he can't believe his eyes. He then flips himself into the church's garbage dumpster. When he rises back up, he has on the suede hat, suede coat, gold chain, diamond cuff-links, diamond watch, diamond ring and the alligator shoes.

The Bum
In my search, I have found my gold and my diamond, but there's still something lacking. I must go into the house of the Lord to see what I am missing.

He goes around to the front of the church and goes in. When he comes in, they greet him and say to him:

Saint
Welcome home and may I ask what is your name?

The Bum
Mr. McClinton; Mr. J. C. McClinton at your service.

Daniel and Donna look over at him and just smile. The service starts. David gets up and walks to the microphone. He opens the service with prayer. He prays that God's heart be shown tonight in the service. He then goes into a song about bowing down on your knees before the Lord. The limousine pulls in front of the church. The driver gets out of the car and opens the back door for the three brothers to come out. The three brothers get out of the car and they say to the driver:

3 Brothers
We thank you and the governor for all that you've done for us. Tell the governor that he definitely has our vote in

The Making of a Prophet

the next election.

The driver says to the three brothers:

Driver
Just remember the governor in your prayers, because he has a hard job to do.

The three brothers say to the driver:

3 Brothers
We will.

Then they shake hands. The driver gets back into the limousine and drives off. The three brothers step inside the church. When they enter the sanctuary, David sees them and says:

David
Come up front.

They come up front where David is and greet one another. The three brothers join in with David singing the song "*Bowing the Knee Before the King*" as they all say together, "for he is the King of glory." After the song ends, everyone begins to clap their hands and thank the Lord. Then the three brothers come down off of the podium where David is standing. Donna grabs hold of Daniel's hand and they begin to make their way up to the front to get a better look at David, for he has their features. They look at him and they begin to weep. Then they turn and begin to walk away with their heads hanging down. David sees them weeping and walking away, then he says to the woman:

David
Woman, are you my mother?

Then he says to the man:

David
Man, are you my father?

David goes down to where they are and puts his arms around them and says:

David
I forgive, I forgive, I forgive you.

David, his father and mother are united in a tearful embrace. David then looks up towards heaven and says:

David
Thank you, Lord. Thank you. Thank you, Lord for answering my prayer.

Pastor John, First Lady Elisabeth, and all the congregation are very emotional at this powerful moment of reconciliation and reunification. There's not a dry eye in the house. They are weeping and praising God saying:

Saints
Thank you Lord, for your mercy endures forever.

Meanwhile, one of the guards at the prison says to the guard that was over the three brothers:

Steve
You gave the three brothers a hard time.

The guard that was over the three brothers says:

Joseph
I know.

He walks away and gets on his phone and says:

> **Joseph**
> Emma, I have done what you asked me to do.

Emma says to the guard:

> **Emma**
> You didn't tell them that you were their father did you?

The guard says to Emma:

> **Joseph**
> No. I did what you asked me to do. Will I ever see you again? The reason I left home ...I was involved in an armed robbery. They arrested me and gave me thirty years. But I made parole at ten years. They even let me work here as a guard and I've been here ever since. I know how you must have felt when you heard my message on your answering machine, after I had been gone from you and our children for sixteen years. All I can say is that I'm sorry. I just want to let you know I'm not the same person I used to be. When that young preacher was out here preaching to our sons, I kneeled down and gave my life to Jesus. Do

>Henry F. Butler, Jr.
>you think we could have dinner sometime?

Emma says to the guard, her husband:

>**Emma**
>Yes Joseph. I would like to have dinner with you sometime. Our three sons, Joseph, Jr., Paul, and our youngest son, Peter, had gotten out of control, but you tried, even though they were in prison, to put them back in order. Your sons and I are still proud to be Johnsons.

Emma's husband, Joseph, simply says to her:

>**Joseph**
>Thank you.

Joseph hangs up the phone, and Steve says to him:

>**Steve**
>You know what I just heard?

Joseph replies:

>**Joseph**
>No. What did you just hear?

Steve says to Joseph:

>**Steve**
>I heard that the governor's driver drove the three

brothers to Welcome Home Church over at 221 Mount Street, and now the governor wants them to work for him as his personal assistants. It's strange how things are going on around here.

Joseph says to Steve:

Joseph
Man it's not strange...that's God! By the way, what time is it?

Steve answers:

Steve
Man, it's 7:05. You are five minutes past your time for getting off.

Joseph replies:

Joseph
Man, I will see you later.

Joseph rushes off from work, gets into his car, and calls Emma from his cell phone. The doors of the Welcome Home Church open once again. However, this time it's Joseph and Emma coming in. The members greet Joseph and Emma by saying:

Saints
Welcome Home!

Joseph responds:

> **Joseph**
> You just don't know how good I feel to be back home.

Joseph and Emma look around the church and they see their three sons just praising the Lord. They walk over to where they are, and when the sons see the prison guard, they say to him:

> **3 Brothers**
> Man, did you follow us even to the church to give us a hard time here also?

Emma says to their sons:

> **Emma**
> There is a reason why he treated you that way. He's your father.

> **3 Brothers**
> What!

> **Joseph**
> All I can say is that I'm sorry for being out of your lives for so long. I'm sorry.

Joseph breaks down and begins to cry. The three brothers look up at their father and say:

> **3 Brothers**
> Welcome home, dad. Welcome home!

Then they all embrace one another. The glory of the Lord has filled the church. Tears of joy are flowing. Everyone has their hands lifted up praising the Lord. God speaks to David and says:

Voice of God
In your humbling, God has been magnified and God has been exalted. Look around and see the glory of the Lord.

The End